Original title:

Forest Follies

Copyright © 2025 Creative Arts Management OÜ
All rights reserved.

Author: Derek Caldwell
ISBN HARDBACK: 978-1-80567-219-7
ISBN PAPERBACK: 978-1-80567-518-1

Bouncing Beams of Sunlit Laughter

Squirrels dance on branches high,
Chasing shadows as they fly.
Bunnies bounce with cheerful grace,
In a sunlit, playful race.

Frogs wear hats of leaves so green,
Jumping to a merry scene.
Birds chirp tunes of silly fun,
Underneath the golden sun.

Mice march in a tiny parade,
With acorn caps, they're all displayed.
Laughter echoes through the air,
In this joyous, wild affair.

The Giggling Gnomes

Gnomes with hats so tall and bright,
Dancing wildly late at night.
Clapping hands, they sing out loud,
Joyful antics make them proud.

With each step, they trip and fall,
Landing softly, giggles call.
Twirling round in silly stacks,
Growning laughter fills the cracks.

Whispers float on midnight breeze,
Wodden shoes and swaying knees.
Under stars, they spin and sway,
In a don't-need-to-be-proper way.

Mischief Amidst the Maples

Maples rustle, leaves conspire,
With little sprites who never tire.
Poking fun at all they see,
Chasing shadows, wild and free.

Acorns rolling down the hill,
Chasing after, thrill by thrill.
Frolicking in playful jest,
Creating chaos, they're the best!

Fawns have joined the merry fray,
With tiny prances, they display.
The giggles bounce from tree to tree,
Embracing all in pure glee.

An Invitation to the Thicket Tea Party

Come one, come all, to a tea so grand,
Where critters gather, hand in hand.
Mice with muffins, badgers with pie,
Laughter fills the air up high.

Daisies serve as fancy plates,
While gossip blooms, and joy creates.
Sips of dew and cookies sweet,
Surrounding each, the day's a treat.

Each guest tells a joke or two,
Of flying frogs and skies so blue.
What a party, who wouldn't say?
Join us for this fun-filled day?

Unruly Growths and Woodland Glee

Amidst the thicket, laughter soars,
A squirrel dons a hat, he explores.
Mushrooms dance in a circle close,
While trees wiggle to the music's prose.

A rabbit in a tie prances with flair,
Chasing a beetle, unaware of the snare.
The wind whispers secrets, soft and spry,
As acorns giggle, drifting by.

Capers of the Hidden Denizens

A raccoon juggles nuts with glee,
A fox twirls 'round a tall birch tree.
Owl plays chess with a passing bug,
While fireflies knit in the warmest snug.

The hedgehogs burst into song so bright,
Hosting a party deep in the night.
Laughter echoes from rock to tree,
In whispers of joy, wild and free.

The Playful Symphony of the Grove

Chirping crickets keep the beat,
As chipmunks tap their little feet.
The brook giggles with a splash so light,
While stars peek out, twinkling bright.

A mouse in a cape leaps on a stone,
Gleefully prancing, never alone.
Branches sway with a merry cheer,
In this merry place, filled with cheer.

Starlit Serenades and Forgotten Paths

In the moonlit evenings, mischief flows,
A raccoon serenades with a nose that glows.
Behind the bramble, a dance breaks out,
Foxes in top hats, jumping about.

The path is lined with winks and grins,
Where every step leads to whimsical spins.
Tales of wonder twist and cheer,
In this playful land, all is dear.

Unruly Roots

In the garden, roots do dance,
Twisting underfoot, they prance.
A carrot trip, a potato slip,
Who knew dirt could be such a lark?

They tangle up in knots so tight,
While worms giggle in delight.
A radish bump, a turnip turn,
Oh, the chaos we all discern!

The Mirth of the Marigold Meadow

Marigolds wear hats of gold,
With giggling petals, brave and bold.
Honeybees buzz with a silly twist,
A dance-off blooms, can't be missed!

The daisies cheer, wild and free,
As bees and blooms share a cup of tea.
"Two sugars please!" the flowers shout,
While butterflies whirl about.

Chasing Shadows by the Streams

By the stream, shadows play tag,
With a flick and a flop, they wag!
Frogs leap over with a croak,
While fish giggle at every joke.

The sunlight joins, a radiant grin,
As antics splash, a splashy spin.
A turtle drops in, makes a splash,
And the ripples dance in a funny flash!

Treetop Tunes and Tumbling Tales

High in the treetops, squirrels sing,
Chasing tales of strange old things.
A nutty drop, a laughter loud,
Woodpeckers tap, they're quite the crowd.

Branches sway in a jolly beat,
While acorns roll beneath their feet.
An owl hoots a riddle wise,
And all the leaves burst into sighs.

Giggling Across the Underbrush

In the underbrush, whispers creep,
Tiny critters laugh, not a peep!
A squirrel tumbles, nuts in flight,
Bouncing off leaves, what a sight!

Frogs don bow ties, all in green,
Practicing jumps for the big screen,
A raccoon sings to the moonlit tide,
While hedgehogs dance, full of pride!

Woodland Whimsy Unleashed

A rabbit hops in too much haste,
But trips on roots, it's quite the waste!
Caught in a thicket, tangled tight,
It giggles softly, what a plight!

Owl wears glasses, oh so chic,
Requesting silence, but can't help a squeak,
The deer in tuxedos prance about,
With laughter echoing, there's no doubt!

Rambunctious Roams in the thicket

Bouncing through brambles, a curious hare,
Clutching wildflowers, none can compare,
A raccoon juggles acorns in the night,
With every drop, it's a pure delight!

Chipmunks host games, all in a row,
Twirling and tumbling, high and low,
When a sleepy bear joins with a yawn,
They all start laughing, until the dawn!

Laughter Beneath Leafy Canopies

Under the leaves, where shadows play,
Fungi dance in a comical way,
A woodpecker mimics a tap-dancing show,
While down below, ants form a row!

Bees buzz tunes, a sweet serenade,
While butterflies twirl in a grand parade,
With every flutter, a chuckle or two,
Nature's own folly, all bright and new!

The Hidden Hoot of the Owl

In the night, a hoot does bloom,
A midnight clown in a tree's costume.
He swivels, twirls, and makes a face,
In the silver light, he finds his place.

With a wink and a flap, he begins to tease,
Scaring the bunnies, rustling the leaves.
A dance of shadows, puffs of air,
What a wild party, all unaware!

Wandering Through Woodland Whimsy

Leaves are giggling, trees are swaying,
In this realm, the critters are playing.
A squirrel juggles acorns with flair,
While the raccoon steals snacks from a dare.

Twisting paths with mischief abound,
The shadows chuckle at those who are found.
Every step's a leap into glee,
In this zany arcadia, wild and free!

Secrets of the Singing Saplings

Tiny trunks with voices bright,
Whispering secrets into the night.
Quirky tunes that tickle the air,
Each note a story, without a care.

Sprouting giggles with every breeze,
A festival of whispers among the trees.
Dancing branches, oh what a sight,
Singing trees with all their might!

The Tantalizing Tangle

Vines and branches weave a web,
A wild puzzle, a playful ebb.
Critters tumble, twirl, and spin,
In this junction, there's no way to win!

Daring escapes and hilarious falls,
Laughter echoes, through the halls.
Caught in a knot, but what the heck,
Life's a comedy, just check your neck!

Autumn's Amusing Antics

Leaves tumble down with a giggle,
Squirrels dart, donning their wiggle.
Pumpkins grinning, all aglow,
Nature's jesters put on a show.

Chirping crickets play their tune,
Rabbits dance beneath the moon.
Acorns bounce, a playful game,
In this woodland, none are the same.

Windy whispers stir the trees,
Rustling laughter on the breeze.
Frolicking critters, joyous shout,
As autumn's antics bring about.

Mushrooms chuckle on the ground,
Pinecones tumble all around.
In this realm of silly cheer,
Every creature holds its beer!

The Jests of Junipers

Junipers chuckle, shaking snow,
In their shadows, gnomes steal the show.
Caterpillars wiggle with glee,
Painting the branches in jubilee.

Berries roll, a squishy prank,
While owls wink from their leafy bank.
Froggy croaks join the leafy jest,
Every moment feels like a quest.

Pine needles tickle the wayward hare,
Who hops around without a care.
Breezes carrying secrets sprightly,
The woods dance wildly, oh so lightly.

Laughter echoes through the wood,
Every creature knows it's good.
In the gnarled branches up so high,
The junipers wink with a twinkling eye!

Melodies of the Midnight Meadow

Fireflies twinkle, lighting the night,
Crickets play tunes, a lovely sight.
Under the stars, grasshoppers leap,
Laughter echoes, waking the sheep.

Moonbeams prance on the silvery dew,
A raccoon serenades with a mew.
Mice in bow ties dance around,
To a symphony of silly sound.

Flowers join with a fragrant cheer,
As the owl hoots, "Let's have a beer!"
Under the glow of the dreamy skies,
All the animals share joyful cries.

In this meadow of night's delight,
Every shadow dances in the light.
Musical antics, the air they weave,
In this midnight, we laugh and believe!

Squirrels' Secret Symphony

Squirrels scurry, tails held high,
Conducting chaos as they fly.
Chirruping melodies fill the glen,
Nutty notes from tail to pen.

Each leap is met with a quack and cheer,
Beneath the beech, the fun is near.
Dancing dandelions join the spree,
A secret symphony, just wait and see.

Fluffy cheeks, a nutty stock,
Composing tunes on the old tree block.
Chipmunks join in with feathery grace,
Creating music in this playful space.

Under the branches, harmonies blend,
Nature's laughter, a comical trend.
In this concert of joy and play,
The squirrels dance the night away!

Dance of the Sylvan Shadows

In the moonlight, shadows prance,
Trees sway in a silly dance.
Squirrels in tiny tuxes twirl,
While the owls hoot and whirl.

Branches wave like crazy arms,
Chasing dreams with woodland charms.
Rabbits wear their best bow ties,
As fireflies light up the skies.

A raccoon starts to DJ soon,
Bopping under the silver moon.
All critters join in the fun,
Echoing giggles, one by one.

Amidst the games and frolic free,
They guffaw as they climb a tree.
Each rustle holds a joyous tease,
Where laughter flows just like the breeze.

Serenade of the Ancient Trees

Tall and wise, the trees will croon,
Tales of mischief under the moon.
Branches creak with every joke,
As leaves giggle with every poke.

Roots dance low to the gentle ground,
Promising fun all around.
A woodpecker's beat, off-key,
Yet every critter sings with glee.

Vines twist, tying up a hare,
While the deer laugh without a care.
The rustling leaves, a playful plot,
Laughter erupted from every spot.

Their ancient voices, full of cheer,
Whispering secrets for all to hear.
In this zany, leafy spree,
Nature's concert plays endlessly.

Laughter in the Leafy Canopy

High above, the branches sway,
Squirrels giggle throughout the day.
A woodpecker taps to the beat,
While chipmunks shuffle their tiny feet.

The sunbeams tickle the blooming flowers,
Making daisies dance for hours.
Underneath, the frogs croak loud,
Their antics drawing quite the crowd.

Each acorn seems to have a tale,
Of runaway bucks and silly snails.
With whispers shared on every breeze,
The canopy hums with sweet unease.

Through laughter echoes, the branches entwine,
As critters gather for fun divine.
Nature's joy, a lively spree,
In leafy laughter, wild and free.

Secrets Beneath the Bark

Underneath the thick brown skin,
Woodland whispers make a din.
Tiny bugs with funny hats,
Reveal their secrets, oh! Just chats.

A worm wiggles in playful glee,
Telling tales of who's the bee.
Ants march in a comical line,
Uncovering snacks that taste just fine.

Mice gossip about the moonlight,
While shadows play, what a delight!
Every crevice has a joke,
Mysteries that beg to poke.

So beneath this wrinkled veil,
Nature's laughter cannot fail.
In every nook, a tale's embark,
With silly secrets lost in bark.

Whispers of the Woodland

Beneath the branches, critters scurry,
A raccoon in a hat looks so very blurry.
Squirrels gossip, tails twitch and flip,
While a fox juggles acorns, losing his grip.

Mushrooms play hide and seek, oh so sly,
While butterflies giggle as they flutter by.
A wise old owl hoots a silly joke,
And even the trees join in with a poke.

Bunnies in bowties host a tea for two,
And frogs croak their thoughts in a silly to-do.
The pinecones fall, causing laughter to swell,
As the woodpecker taps out a comical spell.

In the dappled light, joy bounces around,
Where every twig holds secrets abound.
The woodland is wild with laughter and cheer,
In this playful embrace, all creatures draw near.

Chasing Shadows Among Trees

In the sunlit glade, shadows leap and prance,
A jackrabbit wearing shoes starts to dance.
The shadows giggle, play tag and tease,
While the bushes chuckle at antics like these.

A deer in a tutu spins round and round,
As butterflies laugh at the sight they've found.
A hedgehog in sneakers zips here and there,
While the mischievous gnomes pull their wild hair.

Old trunks become thrones for dandelion kings,
Who rule over laughter and all joyful things.
The owls roll their eyes at the antics below,
While raccoons applaud with a jubilant glow.

As darkness descends, the shadows take flight,
With giggles and whispers to fill the cool night.
The forest alive with a humorous chase,
In this playful realm, there's always a space.

The Secret Dance of Sylvan Spirits

When moonlight spills over leaf and fern,
The hidden ones gather, their laughter a churn.
They twirl through the thickets, all merry and bright,
As fireflies sparkle, adding to the light.

With hats made of petals and shoes of soft dew,
They glide past the trees, as light-hearted spirits do.
A raccoon conductor leads tunes of delight,
While the owls hoot harmony into the night.

In a circle they gather, all singing with glee,
The wise old willow bends down to see.
As starlit confetti descends from above,
Each twirling leaf whispers sweet songs of love.

With chuckles that drift on a midnight breeze,
Joy wraps around branches, and sways with the trees.
As dawn breaks the revel, their laughter takes flight,
In the heart of the woods, where spirits take flight.

Echoes in the Canopy

Echoes flit through the trees, a funny noise,
As chipmunks hold rallies, rallying their joys.
The branches chuckle, leaves throw a fit,
At the antics of squirrels who just won't sit.

A parrot in glasses speaks tales of old,
While rabbits recount their adventures bold.
With a tap of their paws, the whole woodland rocks,
To the beat of a jest by the slyest of fox.

Acorns are drums, as the woodpecker plays,
The creatures join in with their own silly ways.
The laughter crescendoes, fills up the glade,
Echoes of giggles, in sunlight they wade.

In the canopy high, where the sunbeams dance,
You'll find all the critters, lost in their prance.
So if you stroll by, listen close to the cheer,
For the echoes of laughter will always be near.

Twisted Tales of the Wild

A squirrel wears a tiny hat,
While dancing with a lazy cat.
They play chess on a tree stump,
And giggle at each other's jump.

A bear with a bowtie struts so proud,
While birds above sing nice and loud.
They sip tea from acorn cups,
And trade tales of wild hiccup ups.

A raccoon plays the tambourine,
As trees sway to the joyful scene.
A frog joins in, he can't resist,
Grooving with a twirly twist!

The moon peeks in with a cheeky grin,
As shadows dance, they all spin.
They laugh and cheer, oh what a sight,
In the wild, where time takes flight.

Nature's Games in Timeworn Glades

In the glade, the mushrooms grow,
Where rabbits hop to and fro.
They play hide-and-seek with a fox,
While owls count, perched on rocks.

A hedgehog rolls down the hill,
Chasing butterflies, oh what a thrill!
They race past trees, round and round,
Till they trip over leaves that sound.

The wind brings whispers, soft and low,
Tickling the grass, putting on a show.
A gopher pokes its head out wide,
Squeaking jokes and giggling with pride.

As the sun sets with vibrant hues,
The critters gather, singing blues.
With swaying tails and laughing hearts,
Their joy in the glade never departs.

Joyride Through the Timberline

A deer in glasses takes a ride,
On a skateboard, with great pride.
He zooms past trees with a wink,
Sipping nectar from a drink.

The bunnies hop in a line so neat,
Chasing after his quickened feet.
They twist and turn with joyful cheer,
Around each tree, then disappear.

A bear in a helmet joins the spree,
Zooming down the hill, oh so free!
They laugh as they tumble and roll,
In the wild, where fun takes its toll.

The sun dips low with a playful glow,
As giggles ripple, to and fro.
Every critter joins the ride,
In nature's bliss, they all collide.

The Art of Swaying Shadows

In the twilight, shadows play,
Bouncing softly, swaying away.
A fox tiptoes, trying to blend,
In a world where giggles ascend.

The owls hoot in rhythmic beats,
As rabbits dance on tiny feets.
With every sway, the trees do laugh,
At the silly sight of the woodland staff.

A beaver plays a flute, oh dear,
While a raccoon juggles, drawing near.
They spin and twirl in happy delight,
Creating shadows that wiggle at night.

As stars join in with twinkling eyes,
The night rejoices in its disguise.
In the art of shadowy laughter,
Nature sings with joy, ever after.

Winks from Wildflowers

In sunlit meadows, colors dance,
The daisies giggle, take a chance.
With petals bright, they shake and sway,
And tease the bees to join their play.

A buttercup winks, oh what a sight,
It calls the sun to shine so bright.
The violets whisper, secrets shared,
While busy ants march, none are spared.

Each blossom bows, a subtle jest,
They laugh at bumblebees, at their best.
In quips of yellow, pink, and blue,
Nature's jesters, a colorful crew.

Oh, wildflowers' tricks, a merry spree,
They sprout their jokes with wild glee.
With every bloom, their laughter sings,
In this bright patch, joy takes its wings.

Pranks of the Breezy Boughs

The tree branches wiggle, playful delight,
They snatch the hats of passersby in flight.
With rustling whispers, they plot and scheme,
Each gust of wind, a mischievous dream.

Squirrels dart, with acorn bombs,
They toss and roll, oh, what fun charms!
The owls hoot softly, in fits of mirth,
As branches bend low, tease the earth.

A feathered chorus begins to sing,
With chirps and trills, the joy they bring.
Each fluttering leaf plays a crafty role,
In the game of nature, let laughter stroll.

In the dance of shadows, the trees conspire,
Every swaying limb sparks laughter's fire.
With breezy pranks that lighten the load,
The boughs unite, joyful mischief bestowed.

Secrets Shared Amongst Ferns

Amidst the fronds, whispers unfold,
The ferns share tales, both silly and bold.
Their frilly leaves conceal such fun,
As giggles ripple like rays of sun.

A snail slips by, and the ferns exclaim,
"Dare you to bet, it's never the same!"
With laughable glee, they trade their jest,
In the shade of green, they're truly blessed.

They tickle the toads, who jump in surprise,
While fireflies blink with their tiny lies.
Each rustle simmers with joy and light,
Secrets woven in the soft twilight.

When moonlight drips through the leafy crowd,
The ferns stand tall, both shy and proud.
In their hidden world, humor's alive,
With nature's laughter, where spirits thrive.

Silhouettes Under the Moonlit Sky

Under a glow, shadows prance and sway,
The creatures of night join the playful ballet.
Owls share riddles, a wise-guy troupe,
While crickets serenade the midnight group.

A fox in the thicket, sly and spry,
Tickles the moonbeams as they float by.
The rabbits giggle, their ears drawn high,
As fireflies flicker, like stars in the sky.

Swaying willows lend an ear,
To the whispers of laughter, loud yet near.
With quicksilver notes that dance in the air,
The night is alive with a whimsical flare.

As shadows stretch and yawns are heard,
The moon winks down, mightily stirred.
In the theater of night, the laughter insists,
With each playful shadow, joy's gentle twists.

Riddle of the Rooted Realm

In a land where the trees play tricks,
The squirrels juggle acorns, not sticks.
The mushrooms wear hats, all too grand,
While rabbits conspire to start a band.

The wise old owl calls for a show,
With shadows that dance in the glow.
A riddle unfolds in the slide,
As the plants chuckle and confide.

The gnomes around the pond do sway,
Crafting jokes in their wicked play.
Each vine takes turns with a jest,
In a kingdom where laughter's the quest.

Who tickled the roots? Who gave a shout?
The leaves whisper secrets, no doubt.
With every twist in this playful scene,
Life's a giggle, as silly as it seems.

Capers of the Canopied Creatures

Beneath the leaves, where shadows prance,
The critters gather to laugh and dance.
A hedgehog spins in a dizzying whirl,
While the birds in the branches around him twirl.

The raccoon dons a mask too bright,
Scheming to nab a snack just right.
A game of tag ensues up high,
As chipmunks dart like the clouds in the sky.

With every rustle, there's a plea,
"Join us now, come play with me!"
The treetops echo with glee so sweet,
In this world where every friend's a treat.

As sunlight peeks through tangled vines,
Creatures laugh at the silliest signs.
The joy that fills the leafy air,
Is a treasure none can ever compare.

Moonlit Mischief in the Thicket

Under the moon's watchful eye,
The shadows stretch, and creatures pry.
The fireflies twinkle, a guiding light,
While frogs croak rhythms, a merry sight.

A raccoon wears a shiny spoon,
While the badger hums a cheeky tune.
The turtles race, though quite slow,
It's all in fun, as the night winds blow.

"Who left the snacks?" the wise owl hoots,
"Watch out for those sneaky little roots!"
With laughter echoing through the glade,
Their whimsical antics never fade.

The night unfolds, a tapestry bright,
With giggles and games till dawn brings light.
In this place where the wild things play,
Mischief reigns until the break of day.

Frolics of the Fern-Folk

Among the ferns, where secrets dwell,
The tiny folk weave stories to tell.
With thimble hats and laughter loud,
They gather beneath a leafy shroud.

Each fern a friend, a partner in cheer,
The toadstools nod, "We're glad you're here!"
They play hopscotch on the dampened dew,
Creating splashes, a colorful view.

The nimble nymphs dance round and round,
As the whispers of nature's joy abound.
"Who can twirl on a daisy's petal?"
"Bet I can spin like a jolly kettle!"

With every giggle that floats on the air,
Life blooms freely, a joyous affair.
In this lush world of greens and fun,
The frolics continue till day is done.

Frolics in the Green Embrace

In the thicket, squirrels dance,
Chasing shadows, they take a chance.
A rabbit tricks a sleepy bear,
While giggles echo through the air.

Caterpillars do a wiggly jig,
A snail declares, "I'll win the big!"
With frogs debating silly jokes,
And birds who mimic all the hoax.

The trees sway with a gentle tease,
As winds whisper secrets with ease.
A raccoon pranks a shy old hare,
And laughter lingers everywhere.

Oh, nature's stage is full of cheer,
Where blunders turn to heartfelt jeers.
Every creature plays their part,
In this frolicsome, leafy heart.

Mischief Beneath the Bark

Beneath the bark, a beetle plots,
To steal some sweets, but catches knots.
With tiny legs, he makes a run,
The ants are all out just for fun.

A woodpecker, a mighty king,
Knocks on wood to hear it ring.
While moles giggle, hiding low,
At silly games where no one knows.

A mischievous fox in a cloak of fur,
Starts a game with a tiny blur.
And owls hoot with friendly rage,
As all the critters hit the stage.

With laughter trailing through the night,
Each little prank, a sheer delight.
Beneath the bark, where fun abounds,
The wildest antics know no bounds!

Jests of the Leafy Realm

In the leafy realm, where jesters play,
Each step is met with a comedic sway.
A hedgehog rolls, a tumble so grand,
While butterflies dance, all perfectly planned.

A chattering chipmunk starts a race,
With leaf-powered gliders, they up their pace.
A tortoise shouts, "Hey, I'm not slow!"
But shrieks of laughter keep stealing the show.

The mushrooms giggle in colors bright,
As fireflies flash their funny light.
A chorus of crickets sings off-key,
But who's to judge in this jubilee?

Amidst the branches, fun takes flight,
In clever pranks that feel just right.
The leafy realm, alive with cheer,
Echoes the joy as friends draw near.

Revels at Dusk

As dusk settles, the creatures cheer,
With claps and howls, they bring good cheer.
A party starts with the stars above,
Where mischief blooms and laughter loves.

A firefly leads the merry tune,
While raccoons strut beneath the moon.
The owls hoot in their best attire,
Sharing the tales of their wild desire.

The shadows dance, the breezes play,
As dreams frolic in a playful way.
Critters join in a chaotic spin,
Celebrating life, where laughs begin.

Revels at dusk are never tame,
With a playful spirit, they all claim.
In this woodland, full of surprises,
Every moment bursts with sweet disguises.

Jolly Jingle of the Thicket Creatures

Squirrels dance in their tiny shoes,
Chasing shadows, singing the blues.
Rabbits in hats spin round and round,
While grinning foxes gather 'round.

Bumblebees wear goggles with flair,
Humming tunes in the sun-kissed air.
Woodpeckers tap a merry beat,
As chipmunks glide on tiny feet.

Mice juggle acorns, what a sight!
While hedgehogs roll in pure delight.
Laughing leaves in a breezy whir,
Join the party, a chirpy blur.

Under the stars, the night takes flight,
Creatures twirl in the moon's soft light.
A jolly jingle through thicket trails,
The fun continues, laughter prevails.

Capering Through Canopied Dreams

In the canopy, where sunlight plays,
Treetops whisper in mischievous ways.
A parrot dressed in bright charades,
Sings ballads to the budding glades.

Raccoons in masks spy on the scene,
Planning shenanigans, crafty and keen.
They tumble and roll, all paws and tails,
Creating havoc with mishaps and gales.

Owls hoot jokes, wise yet absurd,
While nightingales croon the funniest word.
A yapping dog claims he's a pro,
But trips on a vine, oh what a show!

Through the branches, the laughter rings,
As critters suit up for wild, wacky things.
In dreamy realms where silly things roam,
Capering merriment feels like home.

Whispers Among the Willows

Willows sway with their tangled hair,
Whispering secrets we love to share.
A frog in a tux hops with class,
While crickets chirp and the shadows pass.

A dragonfly dons a crown made of dew,
Declaring herself the queen of the crew.
Mice toss breadcrumbs up in the air,
Creating games without a care.

A beaver starts building a tall, wild tower,
Dancing and prancing with mischief and power.
A bashful snail peeks from his shell,
Wondering if he might join in as well.

Laughter echoes in the gleaming stream,
While fireflies blink, lighting up the dream.
Together they weave a tale so bright,
Whispers among the willows at night.

The Enchanted Grove

In the grove where the wild things play,
Bears wear pajamas and frolic all day.
Wandering elves with shoes that squeak,
Gossip and giggle, oh what a week!

A raccoon chef burns all the toast,
While squirrels toast marshmallows, they boast.
A hedgehog serves tea from acorn caps,
As rabbits fall over from giggly laps.

Mice in bow ties give speeches of cheer,
Squeaking their dreams for the woodland to hear.
Beneath the moonlight, the laughter swells,
In a woodland party where humor dwells.

Joy and jests in the bright, lush glade,
Where tricks and treats are always displayed.
The enchanted grove is a whimsical place,
Filled with delights that make silly grace.

The Raucous Raspberry Rendezvous

In the glade where berries burst,
Raspberries giggle, quench their thirst,
Squirrels dance with silly glee,
While birds sing out in harmony.

Bouncing bunnies hop around,
With berry pies strewn on the ground,
They snatch and munch, oh what a scene!
While giggling goats steal the cuisine.

As fireflies flash in playful bouts,
The chattering chipmunks join the shouts,
They're feasting wild, a jolly crew,
In this berry bash where fun ensues.

But watch your step, a sneaky prank,
A rabid rasp's a slippery bank,
With laughs and slips, they all fall down,
In berry chaos, they wear a crown!

Bold Beetles and Blithe Moments

In the grass, the beetles boast,
With shiny shells, they dance the most,
Their marching band plays quite a tune,
While keeping time with the afternoon.

A ladybug joins in the fun,
She twirls and spins to feel the sun,
Over puddles, they leap and squeal,
Each moment feels like a playful reel.

Ants wear hats, oversized for sure,
While crickets chirp, forever pure,
They host a ball beneath the tree,
Under the moonlight, wild and free.

But keep an eye on sneaky flies,
Who'll swoop and pluck the party prize,
With laughter echoing through the air,
These moments bold, beyond compare!

Larking with the Leaflets

In autumn's glow, the leaves descend,
They tumble down, around the bend,
With gusty giggles, they sway and twirl,
In a dance that makes the branches whirl.

A clever crow caws out a jest,
As squirrels leap and take a rest,
They jump in piles, a feathery mess,
Each crunching sound, a happiness.

The acorns roll with jolly cheers,
While chipmunks play without their fears,
They toss the nuts, just for a laugh,
In the woodland's cheerful photograph.

Yet soon arrives a gusty peek,
And leaves fly off with a ticklish squeak,
In nature's whimsy, they take to flight,
Laughing along, what a silly sight!

The Absurdity of Autumn's Antics

Beneath the boughs where laughter stirs,
The hedgehogs in their little furs,
They roll in piles of leaves so bright,
While owls hoot jokes into the night.

A raccoon dons a scarf with flair,
As skunks parade without a care,
The crickets chirp, with jokes on loop,
In this absurd but jolly troop.

The pumpkins grin with silly glee,
As squirrels toast with acorn tea,
They juggle nuts, a sight to see,
In this merriment, who could disagree?

But when the wind begins to shout,
The antics change, with playful pout,
The forest shakes with giggles bright,
As nature joins in, pure delight!

A Chorus of Forest Fantasies

The squirrels hold a dance on high,
With acorn hats they twirl and fly.
The rabbits hop with great delight,
While owls wink down from yonder height.

A turtle tried to join the fun,
But carried twice as much to run.
They laughed and cheered, 'Oh, what a sight!'
As critters danced till the very night.

A frog croaked tunes both loud and clear,
And all came close to lend their ear.
The trees clapped branches, swayed side to side,
In this grand jest, they took such pride.

At dawn the laughter slowly wanes,
Yet echoes linger in the lanes.
As night falls down, stars peek and grin,
A funny tale shall now begin.

The Jolly Juniper Jamboree

Beneath the branches, sandwiched snug,
A hedgehog rolls, a plump kind of bug.
The junipers hum a merry tune,
As fireflies twinkle 'neath the moon.

A crafty fox in a shiny coat,
Dances around while trying to gloat.
But slippery snails are out for fun,
And one ran past—oh, what a run!

The raccoons juggle pine cone balls,
While rusty old owls make silly calls.
The laughter echoes through the trees,
As nature's jesters roam with ease.

As night drapes down like a soft shawl,
They gather close, enjoying it all.
In this jolly sprinkle of woodland cheer,
Happiness echoes, loud and clear.

Fables from the Foliage

There once was a mouse with a big top hat,
Who rode on the back of a curious cat.
With a tale of cheese and a wink of an eye,
They raced past the trees and let out a cry.

The porcupines wore shoes made of thorns,
While chipmunks played tunes on their sweet little horns.
They gathered round for a game of tag,
With giggly glee, in their colorful rag.

A bear who thought he was quite the dancer,
Tripped on a log, what a wild prancer!
But laughing brook nearby took the lead,
As rustling leaves joined the playful creed.

When dusk fell soft, tales filled the air,
Of laughter and friends, none to compare.
A fable spun in the bright moonlight,
Of woodland wonders and joyous night.

Playful Petals of the Wildflower

A dandelion puff took to the sky,
With wishes and laughter flitting by.
The daisies giggled in bright sunlight,
As butterflies danced in whimsical flight.

The tulips blushed in colors so bold,
While sunflowers shared secrets untold.
They bloomed together in joyful display,
In a playful play, come what may.

A bumblebee buzzed with a cheeky smile,
Wearing a crown made from petals for a while.
He spun around with dizzy delight,
As wildflowers joined in the cheerful plight.

When nighttime drapes with its starry sheen,
The sweet scent of joy becomes quite the scene.
In the garden realm, laughter shall flow,
As playful petals weave stories aglow.

The Whirling Wisteria Waltz

In the glade, where blooms sway,
Dancing vines have much to say.
A squirrel spins, a bird takes flight,
Wisteria twirls, joy in sight.

Leaves giggle with a gentle breeze,
While rabbits hop with perfect ease.
Laughter echoes through the trees,
Nature's jest, a playful tease.

A snail dons shades, oh what a sight,
His little dance brings pure delight.
The frogs croak tunes in offbeat rhyme,
As flowers sway, they mark the time.

Together we join this merry show,
In a wisteria world, we laugh and glow.
With every spin, the heart takes wing,
In this garden, joy is king.

Glimpses of Greener Giggles

Beneath the trees, a game begins,
Where sunlight dapples, and mischief wins.
A raccoon sneaks with a playful grin,
As hidden spots invite us in.

Ladybugs race on a twiggy track,
While a wise old owl gives them flack.
The bunnies bounce, a comical crew,
In their frolicking dance, we join too.

Caterpillars sporting tiny hats,
Wiggle and jiggle, oh what chitchats!
The petals nod, they can't resist,
Cheering on our leafy jesters' twist.

As the sun sets, the laughter swells,
Among the greens, the whimsy dwells.
With winks and chuckles, the night draws tight,
In this verdant realm, all feels just right.

Sunbeams and Shenanigans

Golden rays peek through the leaves,
As chipmunks plot and nature weaves.
With shadows stretching, the antics start,
From high above to the forest's heart.

Pinecones tumble, squirrels in chase,
In a dizzy dash, they find their place.
The sunbeam dances, flickers and prances,
While dandelions join in the chances.

A woodpecker knocks—a comedic beat,
Tapping away with a rhythm neat.
The daffodils sway in laughter and cheer,
As sunbeam quirks make the joke clear.

At twilight's glow, the fun won't cease,
In our glen, we find sweet release.
With giggles shared beneath the stars,
Joyful mischief is never far.

Capricious Critters of the Canopy

High above, where branches play,
Silly squirrels throw nuts on display.
Monkeys swinging with cheeky flair,
Chasing shadows through the air.

A sloth, though slow, gets swept in cheer,
His lazy antics bring joy near.
With silly grins and playful gazes,
They scamper through the leafy mazes.

The parrots squawk their punchline loud,
While below, a frog leaps, feeling proud.
Leaves rustle with giggles and sighs,
Nature's jesters in playful disguise.

As twilight falls, the laughter glows,
In the canopy where joy freely flows.
Each critter's step, a festive dance,
In the wilds, we take our chance.

Revelations Under the Rubble

Amidst the stones and twigs so small,
A squirrel slips, he starts to fall.
He lands on moss, bounces with glee,
And finds a prize—an acorn, whee!

A hedgehog snickers from the side,
Watching the antics, full of pride.
A vulture cackles, "What a sight!"
As critters gather for delight.

They share their tales of stumbles made,
Of mischief, laughter, never dismayed.
With giggles echoing all around,
In this wild maze, joy is found.

The day unfolds with vibrant cheer,
Each slip and slide brings a new jeer.
In nature's raucous, chaotic ruck,
The strangest tales run amok.

A Chorus of Chattering Critters

The chipmunks chat with furious speed,
While rabbits laugh at a fallen seed.
The owl hoots in a riddled way,
As squirrels prance and bicker all day.

"I saw a flower dance in the breeze!"
Cried one small mouse, "It brought me to my knees!"
While birds exchange tales of near-miss flight,
The drumming woodpecker joins the blight.

With every note and sound anew,
The forest forms a lively crew.
They sing of woes, missteps, and trips,
With chuckles bubbling from tiny lips.

When dusk descends and shadows blur,
The critters calm from their joyful stir.
With a yawn and stretch, another day fades,
Yet laughter lingers in the glades.

Meandering Among the Mushrooms

Beneath the cap of a mushroom grand,
A dancing snail draws quite the band.
With twirls and spins, he steals the show,
While fireflies blink in a luminous row.

A field mouse joins with a playful hop,
To the rhythm of nature, they just can't stop.
Each little step brings giggles and squeaks,
Among the fungi, where mischief peaks.

A frog leaps high, with a ribbit-squeal,
Creating a whirl of chaos surreal.
The mushrooms shake to the tune of the dump,
A chorus of laughter, no room for the slump.

In this patch of wonder, they frolic and play,
With smiles exchanged in the mossy ballet.
When the day wraps up, they settle and rest,
In a snug little nook, each feeling blessed.

The Treetop Tango

Up high where the branches twist and turn,
The critters dance with a joyful churn.
A parrot squawks in a colorful boast,
While a raccoon twirls, it's what he loves most.

A sudden gust sends acorns flying,
The dancers duck as they giggle and sigh.
A butterfly flutters, caught in the mix,
With nimble wings, she shows her tricks.

The chatter grows louder, rhythmical claps,
As woodland creatures create playful japs.
Each twist and lean brings a burst of cheer,
With each loud laugh, they conquer their fear.

As dusk whispers gently through leaves above,
The dance slows down, a sleepy love.
In the Treetop haven, hearts all aglow,
They bow to the night, with a flourish and show.

Whimsy Among the Mossy Stones

Amidst the green and twisting vines,
Old mushrooms wear their purple designs.
A squirrel dances on a log,
While a raccoon plays the role of a frog.

The stones giggle under the weight,
As the ants declare a food debate.
With tiny caps and tiny hats,
They boast of treasures found in spats.

The snails glisten, their shells aglow,
While worms gossip of the seeds they sow.
In the laughter, leaves shake and sway,
The forest revels in its silly play.

Each creature shares a joyful jest,
With every twist, a sudden quest.
In this merry, mossy space,
Who knew chaos could be such grace?

The Gossiping Glade

In the glade where whispers roam,
The critters chatter like they're at home.
A woodpecker tells of the best tree,
While the fox rolls eyes at a bumblebee.

A rabbit claims to know a prize,
A patch of carrots that's fit for the eyes.
Squirrels argue over acorn's worth,
As their tales spread like new-found mirth.

The daisies lean in, catching the news,
As the breezes deliver the forest's views.
Every rustle and creak holds a jest,
In this glade, gossip is truly the best.

So much chatter, they can't hold still,
Even the shadows join in for the thrill.
With each tale spun from humor's thread,
Laughter lingers, just like a spread.

Breezy Banter Beneath the Boughs

Under the branches where whispers twine,
The wind brings jokes as the sun starts to shine.
A parrot squawks with a cheeky grin,
While a fox plots his next little win.

The owls hoot in a rhythmic fashion,
Tickling tales with whimsical passion.
Breezes twist around leaves so light,
As laughter dances out of sight.

A hedgehog jests, adorned in spines,
While turtles trade puns—oh, how time unwinds!
With each rustle, the banter grows,
In this vibrant space, humor flows.

From branch to branch, the laughter leaps,
As sunbeams hop and the forest peeps,
Each moment cherished, how sweet this tune,
Beneath the boughs, we are merry as noon!

Tales of the Twisted Trunks

Beneath the twisted ancient trees,
A family of gnomes shares their stories with ease.
With each knot and bend, a tale unfolds,
Of daring escapades and mischief bold.

A raccoon, dressed in flip-flops, arrives,
Claiming adventures, he truly thrives.
But the owls wisely shake their heads,
As the tales grow tall in their cozy beds.

The trunks chuckle at the antics shared,
While vines weave in, having prepared.
With quirky squabbles and wild sights,
The forest pulses with laughter-filled nights.

So gather close, don't miss the fun,
From twisted trunks, the yarns are spun.
In a world of whimsy, where joy abounds,
The tales keep rolling on merry grounds.

The Merry Mischief-makers

In the woods where squirrels play,
They plot and scheme in a silly way.
With acorns tossed like little bombs,
They giggle and dance in leafy balms.

The rabbits race with speed and glee,
Chasing shadows beneath the tree.
They trip on roots and tumble down,
Wearing nature's best crown of brown.

A raccoon steals a picnic snack,
He runs away, the clever little hack.
Bumping into trees, a chaotic sight,
He grins and winks, a comical fright.

In this realm where laughter rings,
Nature's charm is fit for kings.
They jest and jive 'neath the sunlit boughs,
With every chuckle, the heart simply bows.

Rooted Revelations

Beneath the ground where the worms do wriggle,
Roots tell tales in a whispering giggle.
They stretch and tangle, a dance so grand,
Plotting pranks in their earthy land.

Mushrooms wear caps like hats of style,
Fungi festooned with a cheeky smile.
They spring from the soil with grace and flair,
Welcoming all who wander near there.

The grasses sway, performing a jig,
While ants march in with a tiny big gig.
Each blade of green a storyteller bold,
Whispering secrets, both funny and old.

Life below blooms in whimsical cheer,
As laughter rises, the forest we hear.
A carnival of roots, so clever and sly,
In this hidden world, joy can't deny.

In the Veil of Verdancy

Amidst the leaves, a laughter spills,
As chattering birds parade their thrills.
Each branch a stage, each twig a mic,
They sing their tunes like nature's hype.

A deer slips on a slick mossy stone,
With a startled glance, then quick as a drone.
The frogs all croak, in a banded croon,
While fireflies twinkle beneath the bright moon.

The wind whirls through with a playful sigh,
Teasing the branches, they dance and fly.
A symphony sweet of the silly and bold,
Tales of the woods in mischief retold.

In the veil of green, they skip and sway,
Where nonsense is tradition, come what may.
With chuckles and joy, the heart finds its place,
In a world where each moment brings laughter and grace.

The Enchanted Glade's Laughter

In the glade where the sunshine beams,
A squirrel juggles in fits and dreams.
With nuts and berries flying high,
He giggles aloud, oh my, oh my!

The flowers bloom with a zany twist,
Each petal giddy, they can't resist.
A daisy winks at a hapless bee,
Who buzzes around, so blissfully free.

The gnomes play tricks with shadows and light,
Crafting mischief by day and night.
They chuckle as they skitter about,
With fairy dust, they dance and shout.

In this glade where laughter prevails,
Joy fills the air as merriment sails.
Each creature shares in a quirky delight,
In the heart of the woods, where fun takes flight.

Whimsical Wanderings of the Wild

In the woods where the squirrels play,
They juggle acorns night and day.
A rabbit races with a pair of socks,
While a hedgehog struts, proud in his frocks.

Mushrooms dance beneath the trees,
While butterflies giggle in the breeze.
The raccoons gamble on a fallen log,
And the owls hoot, like a funny dog.

Laughing Leaves in the Breeze

Leaves are chuckling, bright and green,
Whirling about like a lively scene.
A snail wears a hat, so jaunty and grand,
While crickets form a quirky band.

The wind whispers jokes to the bushes and shrubs,
As the beetles break out in silly rub-a-dubs.
A mischievous fox makes a feathery shout,
Oh, what a laugh, in the woodlands about!

Knots and Nonsense in Nature

Among the trunks, tangled tales unwind,
Where knots and giggles are intertwined.
A beaver builds, but misplaces his tail,
While a wise old owl delivers a wail.

The toadstools wobble in jovial glee,
As beetles wear sunglasses, oh haplessly free!
In this world of whimsy, all creatures unite,
In knots and nonsense, let's dance through the night.

The Cheery Chanterelle

A fungus, bright, with a grin so wide,
Invites all critters to join for a ride.
With squirrels in tutus and birds in a choir,
They boast of a party that never will tire.

The breeze carries laughter from tree to tree,
While a gopher performs in a jolly spree.
Each step through the glen, a whimsical chance,
To join in the fun of this fungal dance!

The Curious Case of the Climbing Vines

Vines in a tangle, what a sight,
Climbing higher, reaching for light.
They wrestle and wiggle, a leafy dance,
Lucky birds laugh at their clumsy chance.

One vine trips another with a sneaky twist,
They grapple and giggle, can't be missed.
Bouncing up high, like kids on a swing,
What a rollicking ruckus those green limbs bring!

Their laughter echoes, a rustling sound,
As they spiral and twirl around and around.
Oh, the silly mischief in this green world,
With every sprout, a new joke unfurled.

Tangles and tumbles leave no one quite sad,
Each twist a bright smile, who could be mad?
In a jolly uproar, they fashion their act,
A show of the vines, and that's a fact!

Antics of the Acorn Alliance

Acorns in hats, who wore them best?
Racing on squirrels, a nutty quest.
Hop and scurry, they live with flair,
With every tumble, there's joy in the air.

One acorn slipped, rolled down a hill,
Bounced off a mushroom, oh what a thrill!
Laughter erupted from branches above,
Nature's own jesters, a sight to love.

Their meetings held deep in the old oak,
Sharing tall tales and sunny jokes.
In this nutty group, no one feels blue,
As smiles grow larger with every debut.

Buddies in mischief, what a grand crew,
Who knew acorns could party like you?
With twinkling eyes, they scheme and they play,
Adding a sprinkle of joy to the day!

Trials of the Twisted Undergrowth

In tangled grass, where shadows loom,
A game of hide and seek begins to bloom.
Thorns acting as soldiers, daring and stout,
They guard their territory, without a doubt.

But what's this? A root with a sense of jest,
Trips the brave critters, oh, what a mess!
Laughter erupts from the leaves overhead,
As every small stumble brings giggles instead.

A brave little mouse spots a hole nearby,
It leaps for a wonder, then gives a sigh.
Caught in a tangle, legs all askew,
Oh, the silly fate of the brave and the true.

Yet through all the chaos, hearts stay so bright,
With every blunder, they soar back to flight.
In this wild undergrowth, laughter's the key,
A playful reminder of what joy can be!

Pantomime of the Pinecone People

Pinecone folks, dressed in nature's best,
Put on a show, it's a raucous fest.
They shuffle and sway, oh what a scene,
With delicate hats, and chests puffed out keen.

One tries to dance, but wobbles around,
Another slips up, rolls right to the ground.
Giggles erupt from the tall, swaying trees,
As pinecone people flail in the breeze.

With laughter as music, they spin and they twirl,
Every little flounce sends leaves in a whirl.
They stumble through laughter, a merry parade,
Celebrating joy in the games that they've made.

So watch the pinecones, their antics so bright,
Bringing sweet smiles from morning to night.
With every blunder, they cheer and they cheer,
In this nutty realm, there's nothing to fear!

Luminous Larks in the Underbrush

In the thicket, bright larks sing,
They giggle and dance, what joy they bring.
Twisting and twirling, they flit about,
They tickle the toadstools, no shadow of doubt.

A rabbit is laughing, lost in a jig,
While whispering winds tease the old, fat pig.
The daisies sway, join in on the fun,
As sparks of happiness twinkle like the sun.

A squirrel flips pancakes high in a tree,
With syrupy dreams as sweet as can be.
They topple and tumble, such playful delight,
As the clever chipmunks sneak off in flight.

With laughter and merriment brightening the air,
In this lively underbrush, all are aware.
The world is a riot, a circus of glee,
Where even the grumpy find room to be free.

Fables of the Woodland Folk

In the depth of the woods where stories are told,
The critters gather, both timid and bold.
With badger in charge and raccoon on the side,
They spin funny tales, full of mirth and pride.

The deer prances in with a bucket of cheer,
While the owls hoot loudly, "C'mon, gather near!"
With paws on their bellies, they laugh 'til they cry,
As a porcupine juggles, oh my, oh my!

A turtle joins in, slow but with flair,
He flops on his shell, "Hey, do I dare?"
The crowd bursts in laughter, the frogs croak along,
In the shade of the trees, they all sing their song.

So legends are forged in the wildness around,
Where critters of every fur and feather abound.
With joy in their hearts and a skip in their feet,
The fables they tell make life so sweet.

Enigma of the Elders

Beneath ancient branches, the wise ones convene,
With tales and with riddles, the air's rich and green.
The elder trees rustle, their secrets unfold,
As whispers of wisdom get warm in the mold.

"Why did the crow sit on the fence?" they muse,
With a chuckle, they wonder, exchanging their views.
The answer is hidden in giggles and grins,
As the morning sun dances, where the laughter begins.

A fox with a riddle, a bear with a pun,
They're weaving their stories, the laughs weigh a ton.
The spider, bemused, spins a web full of care,
As the woodland conspirators shimmer and share.

So tread soft through the shadows, let joy take a chance,
Join the ancients in mirth, let your spirit enhance.
In the grooves of the bark, in the sway of the air,
The enigma of elders is laughter to spare.

The Cheeky Chipmunk's Game

A chipmunk with charm, so spry and so cheeky,
Nabs acorns for fun, oh isn't he sneaky?
He scurries and bounds, with snacks in his cheeks,
While the birds start to gossip, "Look at him peek!"

"Catch me if you can!" he teases the crew,
As he flips with delight, in a whirlwind of hue.
The rabbit and fox join in on the chase,
While the old tree trunk chuckles, filling the space.

With darting and dodging, what playful pursuit,
He dances through thickets, oh, what a hoot!
"A nibble for you if you can keep up!"
But the friends just roll over, all giggling, "Wup!"

As dusk meets the dawn, their laughter will ring,
In the game of the day, it's the joy that they bring.
The chipmunk, triumphant, he grins ear to ear,
For laughter's the treasure, the best of all cheer.

The Jive of the Jasmine

Jasmine danced with a jitterbug sway,
While bees took flight with a humorous play.
Brought their friends for a buzzing parade,
Swaying petals in a fragrant charade.

A butterfly twirled, in polka dot pride,
Caught in the music, there's nowhere to hide.
The sunlight chuckled, its rays in the mix,
As flowers all blended those silly quick tricks.

Squirrels in bow ties, on branches they spun,
Chasing their tails, oh what silly fun!
A rabbit played drums, with an acorn he found,
In this jive of jasmine, all giggles abound.

And when the day ended, they danced out of sight,
Under the stars, in a shimmering light.
The fragrance still lingers, a whimsical scent,
In a jasmine jive, where the chuckles were spent.

Enchantment of the Elder Boughs

In the elder's embrace, where whispers are spun,
An owl cracked a joke, what a hoot, oh what fun!
The branches, they creaked, in a symphonic sway,
As critters all chuckled through the warm autumn day.

A fox in a coat tried to sneak up with pride,
Tripped on his tail, and the whole woods just sighed.
The laughter could echo, the trees all would sway,
With secrets shared softly in their leafy ballet.

A pair of young raccoons, in mischief they'd bask,
Wore moss as a hat, on a comical task.
They rummaged for snacks, in the root of the old,
Finding acorns and berries, a treasure untold.

As twilight descended, the stars blinked awake,
The elder's sweet laughter was hard to mistake.
In the heart of the grove, where enchantments would blend,
The boughs would keep secrets, and chuckles, my friend.

The Spirited Sagebrush Soirée

Sagebrush gathered for a grand little fête,
With cacti in costumes, oh what a sight!
Under moonlight's charm, the spirits danced bold,
With every long shadow, a tale to be told.

A lizard in ledgers marked dates with a smile,
Gossiping softly, they jived for a while.
While wind played the tune in a playful refrain,
The coyote howled back, like the wildest of trains.

The stars twinkled bright in a cheeky soft glow,
As tumbleweeds rolled in with a laugh, "Let's go!"
A roadrunner raced, with a wink in his eye,
"Can't catch me!" he teased, as he zipped on by.

The night wore on sweet, with cactus drinks sipped,
Each moment a spark, with delight, it was scripted.
Such antics and joys, in the sagebrush soiree,
Where laughter is golden, and worries decay.

Mischief in the Meadow's Heart

In the meadow's embrace, where wildflowers bloomed,
Bunnies and badgers made mischief assumed.
With hops and with snickers, they dashed to and fro,
Their giggles like breezes, oh how they would blow!

A squirrel in a hat, born of dandelion,
Juggled sweet acorns with wild style, undying.
While chipmunks all cheered for their friend in the air,
As daisies blushed pink, oh the joy was quite rare!

The sun played along, with a wink from above,
Tickling the petals, like an old friend in love.
And in shady spots, where the tall grasses lay,
The whispers of laughter danced soft through the day.

As dusk painted skies, in hues of delight,
The meadow tucked in all its fun for the night.
With dreams full of pranks, and giggles anew,
In the heart of the meadow, the mischief just grew.

www.ingramcontent.com/pod-product-compliance
Lightning Source LLC
Chambersburg PA
CBHW051629160426
43209CB00004B/573